D1569626

Zoom In on
Trailblazing Athletes

Muhammad Ali

Jennifer Strand

abdopublishing.com

Published by Abdo Zoom™, PO Box 398166, Minneapolis, Minnesota 55439. Copyright © 2017 by Abdo Consulting Group, Inc. International copyrights reserved in all countries. No part of this book may be reproduced in any form without written permission from the publisher. Abdo Zoom™ is a trademark and logo of Abdo Consulting Group, Inc.

Printed in the United States of America, North Mankato, Minnesota
072016
092016

Cover Photo: Dan Grossi/AP Images
Interior Photos: Dan Grossi/AP Images, 1; AP Images, 4, 5, 7, 10, 11, 15, 16; John Lent/AP Images, 8; Central Press/Getty Images, 9; GS/AP Images, 12; Phil Sandlin/AP Images, 19

Editor: Brienna Rossiter
Series Designer: Madeline Berger
Art Direction: Dorothy Toth

Publisher's Cataloging-in-Publication Data
Names: Strand, Jennifer, author.
Title: Muhammad Ali / by Jennifer Strand.
Description: Minneapolis, MN : Abdo Zoom, [2017] | Series: Trailblazing athletes
    | Includes bibliographical references and index.
Identifiers: LCCN 2016941526 | ISBN 9781680792522 (lib. bdg.) |
    ISBN 9781680794205 (ebook) | 9781680795097 (Read-to-me ebook)
Subjects: LCSH: Ali, Muhammad, 1942- --Juvenile literature. | African American
    Boxers--Biography--Juvenile literature. | Boxers (Sports)--United States--
    Biography--Juvenile literature.
Classification: DDC 796.83092 [B]--dc23
LC record available at http://lccn.loc.gov/2016941526

Table of Contents

Introduction

Muhammad Ali was one
of the best boxers ever.

He won many championships. He also led **social change**.

Early Life

Ali was born on January 17, 1942. His birth name was Cassius Clay. He started boxing when he was 12.

Rise to Fame

Clay trained a lot. He won 100 fights in six years. In 1960 he went to the Olympic Games.

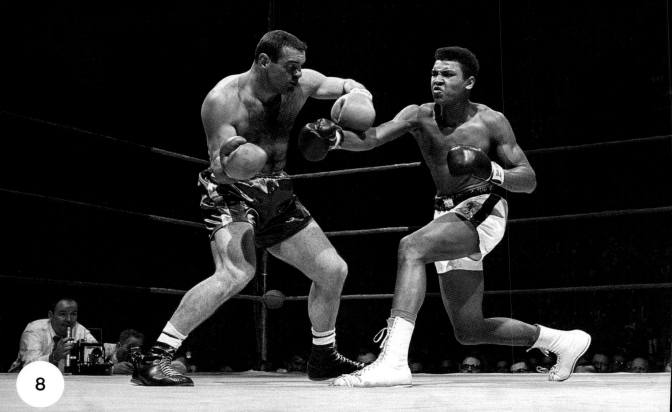

He won a gold medal.

Clay won the world
heavyweight title in 1964.

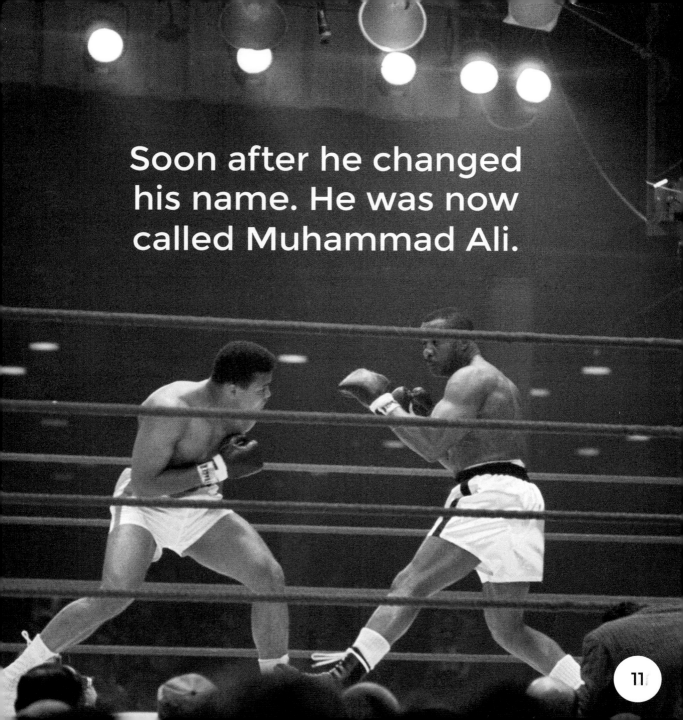

Soon after he changed his name. He was now called Muhammad Ali.

History Maker

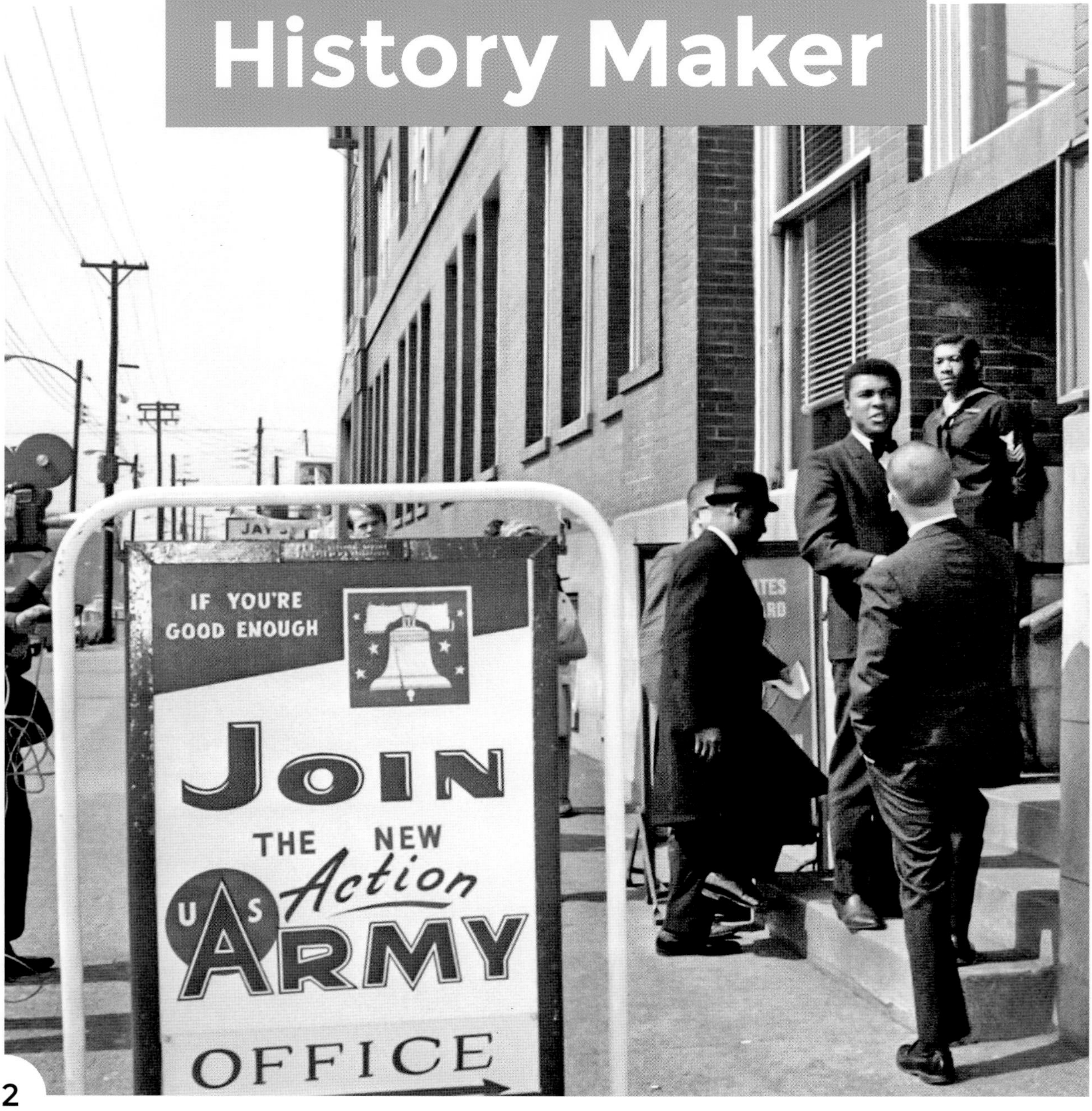

In 1967 Ali refused to fight in the Vietnam War (1954–1975). He was **banned** from boxing because of this. Many people were mad at him. Others respected his decision.

Ali boxed again more than three years later. He beat many great boxers. He became the heavyweight champion two more times.

He was one of the most famous **athletes** in the world.

Legacy

Ali often bragged about his skills. He called himself "the greatest."

He also made his words **rhyme**. People liked to hear what he would say. This helped make him very famous.

Ali **retired** from boxing in 1981. He had Parkinson's disease. But he kept working to help people. He also tried to make boxing safer.

On June 3, 2016, he died.

Muhammad Ali

Born: January 17, 1942

Birthplace: Louisville, Kentucky

Sport: Boxing

Known For: Ali was a champion boxer and social leader.

Died: June 3, 2016

Key Dates

1942: Cassius Marcellus Clay Jr. is born on January 17.

1960: Clay wins an Olympic gold medal and his first pro fight.

1964: Clay wins the world heavyweight title. He also joins the Nation of Islam and takes the name Muhammad Ali.

1970: Ali returns to the ring after 43 months. He wins his first fight.

2005: Ali is awarded the Presidential Medal of Freedom.

2016: Ali dies on June 3.

Glossary

athlete - a person who plays a sport.

banned - kept from using or doing something.

retired - finished a job and not working anymore.

rhyme - when words or phrases end in the same sound.

social change - a change in the way people in a community think, act, or treat each other.

Booklinks

For more information
on **Muhammad Ali**, please visit
booklinks.abdopublishing.com

 **In on Biographies!**

Learn even more with the Abdo Zoom
Biographies database. Check out
abdozoom.com for more information.

Index